Sports Illustrated KIDS

ATHLETES FOR
RACIAL EQUITY

JACKIE ROBINSON, ARTHUR ASHE, AND MORE

by Sibylla Nash

CAPSTONE PRESS
a capstone imprint

Published by Capstone Press, an imprint of Capstone.
1710 Roe Crest Drive, North Mankato, Minnesota 56003
capstonepub.com

SPORTS ILLUSTRATED KIDS is a trademark of ABG-SI LLC. Used with
permission.

Library of Congress Cataloging-in-Publication Data is available on the Library
of Congress website.
ISBN: 9781663966001 (hardcover)
ISBN: 9781666321340 (paperback)
ISBN: 9781666321357 (ebook pdf)

Summary: Jackie Robinson was the first Black player in Major League Baseball.
Arthur Ashe was the first Black man to win several pro tennis titles. Readers will
learn about these athletes and others who have fought for and spoken out for racial
equity in sports and the greater society.

Image Credits
Alamy: Hirarchivum Press, 7; AP Photo, 4, 6, 26, Kevin Rivoli, 19, Lana Harris,
27; Getty Images: John Moore/Staff, 20, The Asahi Shimnun, 17; Newscom: ALFO
SPORT/Yohei Osada, 23, Image of Sport/Kirby Lee, 25, Sporting News Archives/
Icon SMI, 5, ZUMA Press/Timothy L. Hale, 22; Shutterstock: Paul Craft, Cover;
Sports Illustrated: David E. Klutho, 29, Erick W. Rasco, 21, John G. Zimmerman,
9, 11, 15, John W. McDonough, 13, Neil Leifer, 24

Editorial Credits
Editor: Erika L. Shores; Designer: Heidi Thompson; Media Researcher: Jo Miller;
Production Specialist: Tori Abraham

All internet sites appearing in back matter were available and accurate when this
book was sent to press.

TABLE OF CONTENTS

Introduction......................................4

Breaking Barriers
and Opening Doors..........................6

Protests and Boycotts.....................14

Activism on Ice 22

Getting the Word Out.....................24

Glossary 30

Read More 31

Internet Sites..........................31

Index....................................32

About the Author 32

Words in BOLD appear in the glossary.

INTRODUCTION

Many fans look at pro athletes as heroes. They are the fastest runners or highest jumpers in the game. Some are heroes in other ways too.

There was a time when certain players were not allowed to compete because of the color of their skin. It did not matter if they were the best at their sport. When they finally were allowed to play, they were not treated the same. This unfair treatment is called racial inequity.

Olympic gold medalist Wilma Rudolph (center) used her fame to bring about changes to her hometown in Tennessee.

Some athletes decided to fight for fairness, or racial equity. They became **activists.** They spoke out against unfair treatment. Over time, activist athletes have taken a stand. They did so even if it meant risking their careers or personal safety.

Jackie Robinson was the first Black baseball player in Major League Baseball (MLB).

BREAKING BARRIERS AND OPENING DOORS

It's not always easy being the first person to do something. This was especially true when **segregation** and Jim Crow laws were in effect. But some famous athletes of color changed that. They helped others swing, run, and dunk their way into the game.

In many cities in the South, signs announced which places were for white people only.

JIM CROW LAWS

Jim Crow were a set of laws from the South based on race. The Separate but Equal law began in 1877. Black people were not allowed to attend the same schools as whites. The laws kept Black people and white people apart at restaurants, swimming pools, gyms, and other public spaces. These laws didn't end until the mid-1960s.

MARSHALL "MAJOR" TAYLOR

Major Taylor went from working in a bicycle shop to becoming a cycling champ. He was the first Black man to **integrate** the sport. He began pro racing at 18 years old in 1896. By 1903, he had won bicycle races all over the world.

Taylor was born and raised in Indianapolis, Indiana. He was kept from racing at a local track because of his skin color. Once he started winning, other racers threatened his life. They tried to get him banned from races. Taylor proved that, when given a fair chance, Black athletes could excel.

Major Taylor during a cycling race

JACKIE ROBINSON

In 1947, Jackie Robinson became the first Black man to play pro baseball in the major leagues. He went on to lead the Brooklyn Dodgers to six World Series appearances and one World Series championship. Robinson led the way for more Black players in MLB. Six more players entered by 1948.

After retiring from baseball, Robinson raised money for the Southern Christian Leadership Conference (SCLC). He held jazz concerts in his backyard. The money raised was used for activists who had been put in jail.

In 1964, Robinson helped start the Freedom National Bank in Harlem. Black people were often kept from taking out loans to start businesses or buy homes. Robinson's bank wanted to change that.

Jackie Robinson was the first Black player inducted into the Baseball Hall of Fame.

ALTHEA GIBSON

Tennis legend Althea Gibson was often called the female Jackie Robinson. She was an athlete of many firsts. For 70 years, Black people were not allowed in the United States Tennis Association (USTA). They had to form their own league and tournaments. That changed in 1950 when Gibson became the first Black person to play at the U.S. Nationals.

Between 1956 and 1958, she became the first Black person to win at Wimbledon and at the U.S. Nationals (now called the U.S. Open). She went on to win 11 Grand Slams. Her talent and determination encouraged other Black athletes.

FACT

Althea Gibson shook the Queen of England's hand after winning at Wimbledon. This was during the time when Black people could not eat at a lot of the same restaurants as white people.

Althea Gibson competing in the U.S. Nationals in 1956

JEREMY LIN

In 2012, "Linsanity" swept the United States. Jeremy Lin was the first American born pro basketball player of Chinese or Taiwanese descent. He helped the New York Knicks turn around a losing season. He scored more points in the first five games he started than Michael Jordan did in his. During that time, *Sports Illustrated* put him on their cover two weeks in a row.

In 2021, there was an increase in **racism** toward Asian people. The COVID-19 global **pandemic** began in China. Many people wrongly blamed Asian people for the virus. Lin spoke out. He also supported the #StopAsianHate campaign on social media.

Jeremy Lin on the basketball court in late 2012

PROTESTS AND BOYCOTTS

Some activist athletes chose to put their careers on the line by sitting out the sport they love. Others took to the streets in protest. Both ways helped bring about change.

WILMA RUDOLPH

Wilma Rudolph was known as "The Fastest Woman in the World." Rudolph became the first American woman to win three Olympic gold medals in track and field. After the 1960 Olympics, she came home to Clarksville, Tennessee. The city wanted to hold a segregated celebration in her honor. But Rudolph said she would not attend. Because of this, the event was changed to include both Black people and white people. It was the first event in her hometown to do so.

Wilma Rudolph winning the 200-meter race in the 1960 Olympics

In 1963, Rudolph was kept out of a Shoney's restaurant in Clarksville. It only served white people. She joined with hundreds of people to protest. Days later, the mayor said restaurants in the city should serve all people.

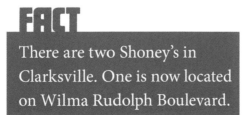

FACT

There are two Shoney's in Clarksville. One is now located on Wilma Rudolph Boulevard.

EROSEANNA "ROSE" ROBINSON

Rose Robinson was a talented track and field high jumper. In 1958, she was named to the National Women's Track and Field team. In 1959, at the Pan American Games, Robinson did not stand for the national anthem. She did this to protest racism. But her activism started years before. In 1952, she led "skate-ins" to integrate a popular skating rink in Cleveland, Ohio. During skate-ins, Robinson brought Black children to skate at the all-white skating rink.

FACT

Rose Robinson was once shoved so hard at a skate-in that she broke her arm.

WYOMIA TYUS

Wyomia Tyus competed in the 1964 and 1968 Olympic Games. She was the first person to win back-to-back gold medals in the 100-meter track and field event. During the 1968 games, she wore a pair of black shorts instead of her required uniform. This was her way of protesting racial injustice.

Tyus later dedicated her medal to teammates Tommie Smith and John Carlos. They were sent home after raising black-gloved fists during the U.S. national anthem. They too were silently protesting racism.

Wyomia Tyus (center) at the start of her race in the 1968 Olympics

SYRACUSE 8

Sometimes doing the right thing can cost a player everything. In 1970, nine Black members of the Syracuse University football team experienced unfair treatment. The coaching staff had been all white since 1898. The Black players had been asking for more than a year for a Black assistant coach. The nine players decided to do something. They made a list of demands. They refused to take part in spring practice unless their demands were met.

Newspapers reported about their demands. They were mistakenly called the Syracuse 8 (although there were nine players). The school was flooded with letters against the Black players. They were removed from the team. Their actions later led to changes in how the school ran its football program. But seven of the nine team members never played for the school again.

In 2006, the Syracuse 8 were honored by the university for taking a stand against injustice.

A LIST OF INEQUITIES

The Syracuse 8 listed several examples of unfair treatment. They said the team doctor didn't want to touch them because they were Black. The Black players also said they received less playing time on the field. Some universities didn't want to play against Black athletes.

NATALIE VIE

Natalie Vie didn't become a **fencer** until she was 18 years old. She tried out for the fencing team at Arizona State University. She landed a spot and later became the team captain. In 2012, she was the first Latina on the U.S. Olympic fencing team.

Vie grew up in Arizona. State laws were being passed to allow **racial profiling**. Vie spoke against these unfair laws. She also wrote about her experiences being Latina.

FACT

Natalie Vie created a cartoon called *Super Sonic Nava*. It featured a Latina superhero and her alter ego.

Natalie Vie in 2014

NATASHA CLOUD

The Washington Mystics won the 2019 Women's National Basketball Association (WNBA) championship. But in 2020, Mystics point guard Natasha Cloud decided not to play. Instead, she focused on her fight against **systemic racism.**

Cloud joined thousands in a protest in Philadelphia. They wanted justice for the murder of George Floyd. Floyd was an unarmed Black man killed by a police officer in Minneapolis. Cloud also wrote a powerful piece about racism. She led a march on **Juneteenth** in Washington, D.C.

Natasha Cloud during a 2019 playoff game

ACTIVISM ON ICE

Few people of color compete at the highest levels in figure skating. Starr Andrews and Elladj Baldè wanted to highlight the lack of people of color in the sport. They used music and videos to do it.

STARR ANDREWS

Starr Andrews glided onto the skating scene at age 9. She posted a video of herself figure skating to Willow Smith's "Whip My Hair." It went **viral**. The video was viewed 56.8 million times. Andrews placed sixth at the U.S. Championships in 2018 and 2020. In 2020, she posted a video of herself skating to Mickey Guyton's "Black Like Me." Andrews used the song to honor the struggles Black Americans face.

Starr Andrews skated in the 2020 U.S. Figure Skating Championships.

ELLADJ BALDÈ

Elladj Baldè went viral in early 2021 after posting videos of himself figure skating. Viewers tuned in 30 million times to watch him flip and spin. The former competitive figure skater wanted people to see a person of color on the ice. His mother is Russian and his father is African. Baldè helped start the Figure Skating Diversity and Inclusion Alliance. Hundreds of members work to make the sport more inclusive for skaters of color.

Elladj Baldè performed in a 2020 figure skating show in Japan.

GETTING THE WORD OUT

Many activist athletes lend time and money to groups and events fighting for causes. Some athletes go even further. They start their own organizations.

BILLY MILLS

Billy Mills (also known as Tamakoce Te'Hila) won a gold medal in the 1964 Olympics. He became the first and only American to ever win the 10,000-meter race. He grew up on the Pine Ridge Indian Reservation in South Dakota. He is a tribal member of the Oglala Lakota Nation.

Mills has spoken out against systemic racism. He said it was wrong for sports teams to use American Indian mascots. Because of this, he has been spit on and called names.

Billy Mills leading the 10,000-meter race in the Olympics in Tokyo, Japan

Mills helped start Running Strong for American Indian Youth. The group provides everyday needs such as running water to homes on reservations. Mills has raised more than $40 million for the organization.

Billy Mills continues to be an activist who speaks out against racism.

ARTHUR ASHE

Arthur Ashe was a tennis great. Ashe is the only Black man to win the singles title at Wimbledon, the U.S. Open, and the Australian Open. He was ranked as the number one U.S. tennis player in 1968. Despite his ranking, Ashe was not allowed to play in a tournament in South Africa. The South African government practiced **apartheid.** They kept Black people and white people apart. Ashe did not give up his fight to compete. In 1973, he became the first Black player to play in South Africa's national championships. He won the doubles title.

Arthur Ashe competing in the South African Tennis Championships in 1973

In 1983, Ashe started Artists and Athletes Against Apartheid. They organized a group of athletes and entertainers who refused to perform in South Africa. In 1985, Ashe was arrested at an anti-apartheid protest in Washington, D.C.

Arthur Ashe (right) was arrested and handcuffed along with other protesters outside the South African Embassy in Washington, D.C., on January 12, 1985.

CARMELO ANTHONY

Carmelo Anthony is a four-time Olympian. The Puerto Rican and African American athlete has won three gold medals and one bronze in basketball. In 2013, the NBA star helped lead the New York Knicks to a division title for the first time in 19 years. Off the court, Anthony is also known for speaking out against racism.

Anthony leads by example. In 2015, he marched in Baltimore. People there were protesting the death of a Black man named Freddie Gray at the hands of the police.

Anthony went viral in 2016 with an Instagram post. He called on other athletes to take charge in the fight for racial justice. That same year, he spoke out again. During the ESPY Awards, he addressed racism and police **brutality.** He spoke alongside LeBron James, Chris Paul, and Dwayne Wade. He also joined with other players to create the Social Change Fund. The group's goal is to help build a fair and just society.

Carmelo Anthony shoots the ball during a 2013 playoff game.

GLOSSARY

activist (AK-tiv-ist)—a person who works for social or political change

apartheid (uh-PAR-tide)—the practice of keeping people of different races apart

brutality (broo-TAL-uh-tee)—cruel, harsh, and usually violent treatment of another person

fencer (FEN-sur)—a person who practices the sport of fencing; fencing involves using swords

integrate (IN-tuh-grate)—to bring people of different races together in schools and other public places

Juneteenth (joon-TEENTH)—a holiday that celebrates the news reaching Texas on June 19, 1865, that the Civil War had ended and enslaved people had been freed

pandemic (pan-DEM-ik)—a disease that spreads over a wide area and affects many people

racial profiling (RAY-shuhl PRO-fye-ling)—the use of race or ethnicity as a reason for suspecting someone of having committed a crime

racism (RAY-siz-uhm)—the belief that one race is better than another race

segregation (seg-ruh-GAY-shuhn)—the practice of keeping groups apart, especially based on race

systemic racism (SYS-tem-ik RAY-siz-uhm)—when systems and institutions privilege one race above another

viral (VYE-ruhl)—quickly and widely spread or made popular especially by means of social media

READ MORE

Marcovitz, Hal. *Racial Injustice: Rage, Protests, and Demands for Change.* San Diego: ReferencePoint Press, 2021.

Solien, Paula. *12 Athletes Who Changed the World.* Mankato, MN: 12 Story Library, 2020.

Weintraub, Aileen. *We Got Game: 35 Female Athletes Who Changed the World.* Philadelphia: Running Press Kids, 2020.

INTERNET SITES

Ducksters: Civil Rights for Kids Overview
ducksters.com/history/civil_rights/

Goodsport: Female Athletes Fighting for Social Justice
goodsport.me/female-athletes-fighting-for-social-justice/

Youth Civil Rights Academy: Sports, Activism, and Social Justice
youthcivilrights.org/portfolio_page/sports-activism-and-social-justice/

INDEX

Andrews, Starr, 22
Anthony, Carmelo, 28, 29
Ashe, Arthur, 26, 27

Baldè, Elladj, 22, 23
basketball, 12, 21, 28

Carlos, John, 17
Cloud, Natasha, 21
COVID-19, 12
cycling, 7

fencing, 20
figure skating 22, 23
football, 18

Gibson, Althea, 10, 11

high jumping, 4, 16

Lin, Jeremy, 12, 13

Major League Baseball (MLB), 5, 8
Mills, Billy, 24, 25

national anthem, 16, 17

Olympics, 4, 14, 15, 17, 20, 24, 28

Robinson, Eroseanna "Rose," 16
Robinson, Jackie, 5, 8, 9, 10
Rudolph, Wilma, 4, 14, 15
running, 4, 14, 15, 17, 24

Smith, Tommie, 17
Syracuse 8, 18, 19

Taylor, Marshall "Major," 7
tennis, 10, 26
Tyus, Wyomia, 17

Vie, Natalie, 20

ABOUT THE AUTHOR

Sibylla Nash has written two novels and hundreds of articles for magazines and newspapers. This is her second book for children. She lives in Los Angeles with two bossy cats and shares a love of anime with her daughter.